New Word A Day

365 Computer Terms

Vocabulary Calendar

Elliot Carruthers

ISBN-13: 978-1541200227
ISBN-10: 1541200225

Harddrive

Jan 1

Nice invention! Let's call it a harddrive.

A harddrive is where your data is stored long-term.

UPS

Jan 2

How the UPS got its name.

UPS stands for Uninterruptible Power. A UPS is a battery that keeps your computer running if the power goes out.

Hacker   Jan 3

I think a hacker got my computer!

A hacker is a person who breaks into computers to steal confidential data.

GMail   Jan 4

Thus was born the Gmail name.

Gmail is a free email service provided by Google.

ERP   Jan 5

The ERP system says we have a million thing-a-ma-jigs.

ERP stands for Enterprise Resource Planning. An ERP system is a suite of programs designed to run an entire company.

MRP   Jan 6

We have enough material to make a million whos-ee-whats.

MRP stands for Material Requirements Planning. An MRP system is used to run the manufacturing department of a company.

Query

Jan 7

I never knew how many pets I had until I ran this query.

CATS 23
DOGS 45
TOTAL 68

A query is a command used to get data from a database.

Phablet

Jan 8

My new phablet? It's phabulous!

A phablet is a PHone and a tABLET. You can draw on it and make phone calls.

Dongle   Jan 9

Why do a I need a dongle
to play a video game?

A dongle is a key on a USB stick. You plug it into a
computer to prove you have a software license.

Virtual Reality   Jan 10

This virtual reality feels so real!

Virtual Reality makes you think a video game is real.

Captcha   Jan 11

Captcha means gotcha in French. Kiddn.

Captcha is used to prove you are not a computer trying to access a website.

Bug   Jan 12

The bug problem is getting bad. You need to have less bugs.

A bug is an error in a program.

Bus

Jan 13

The data bus carries data between computers.

Script

Jan 14

I'll let you know when it's done with the script.

A script is a program a computer or a website runs.

CPU   Jan 15

This is the CPU. You can see it's very advanced.

CPU stands for Central Processing Unit. The CPU is the brain of the computer. It is where all the calculations happen.

Driver   Jan 16

Well. I did say get me a mouse driver...

A driver is a small program that tells the computer how to use things you plug into it.

Facetime

Jan 17

My cat loves Facetime.

Facetime is an app for the IPhone that let's two people see each other while they talk.

Cloud

Jan 18

My data is in the cloud and I can get it from anywhere.

The cloud is a remote system you can rent that stores your data.

RAD   Jan 19

Put the box there.
No. Put it there.
Noooo. Hmmm...

RAD stands for Rapid Application Development. RAD is
a development system that uses little documentation
or specifications.

Scrum   Jan 20

I see we finally
hired a Scrum
master.

SCRUM is a way to develop software by having a lot of
meetings.

Cache   Jan 21

No. I said I need more cache. Not cash.

The cache is temporary harddrive space used to store data when your computer runs out of memory.

WORM   Jan 22

So... what inspired you to call your new invention a WORM?

WORM stands for Write Once Read Many. A WORM CD becomes read-only after it is created.

Portal

Jan 23

This is my favorite portal.
I start the day here.

A portal is a customizable website used to launch other websites.

Flash Drive

Jan 24

I bought a new
flash drive.

A Flash Drive is a portable harddrive on a stick that goes in your pocket.

Firewall   Jan 25

A firewall prevents unauthorized people and programs from getting onto your computer.

Surf   Jan 26

You surf the Internet by going from website to website.

Undelete   Jan 27

There. Your files
just reappeared.

In Windows... press the ctrl key and the Z key at the same
time to undo the last command... including delete.

Smartwatch   Jan 28

My smartwatch
also has a grill
and a blender.

A smartwatch does much more than tell the time. It has
a computer and often a phone.

Hotmail   Jan 29

A Hotmail came for you.

Hotmail is a free email service owned by Microsoft.

Malware   Jan 30

Bad malware! Bad!

A malware program pretends to be innocent with the intent of doing something bad on your computer.

CBT   Jan 31

I train everyday with my computer.

CBT stands for Computer Based Training. CBT is a program that presents a topic with a quiz.

Intel   Feb 1

The only thing I found inside... is a dust bunny.

Intel is a company that makes computer chips. Its slogan is "Intel Inside".

Solid State　　　Feb 2

A solid state computer has no moving parts. It is very durable.

Biobreak　　　Feb 3

A biobreak is computer slang for a bathroom break.

Basic

Feb 4

So... your'e our basic programmer!

Basic is a computer lanuage that was for beginners. It stands for Beginner's All-Purpose Symbolic Instruction Code. Professionals use it now.

Wi-Fi

Feb 5

In general... Wi-Fi is when you use the Internet connection of the building you are in.

Wi-Fi stands for Wireless Fidelity.

Architecture Astronaut   Feb 6

You're an architecture astronaut. I only asked you to add two numbers.

Architecture astronaut is slang for a developer who complicates a simple design for a computer program.

Router   Feb 7

Well, son... a router is something you have to restart once in a while.

A router connects a computer to a network.

LOL   Feb 8

Ha ha ha! Lol!

LOL stands for Laugh Out Loud. LOL is used to show laughter in Internet chat or email.

BRB   Feb 9

I'll be waiting.

BRB stands for Be Right Back. BRB is used during texting to tell someone you will be away from your computer for a short time.

Dock   Feb 10

You don't have to make beeping noises when you dock your laptop.

A dock quickly connects a laptop to a monitor and a printer.

FYI   Feb 11

FYI. You're walking around with a rip in the rear.

FYI stands for "For Your Information". FYI is used in chat and email. It's like saying... "to let you know".

NINO   Feb 12

It's blank
because it's a
NINO program.

NINO stands for Nothing In Nothing Out. NINO means
the computer did nothing because it was given nothing.

Attachment   Feb 13

I just got your attachment.
It's very attached.

An attachment is a file you send to someone by
including it in an email.

HTML   Feb 14

It's my first HTML program.
It took me four days to learn.

HTML stands for Hype Text Markup Language. HTML is
a computer language used to build websites.

IMAP   Feb 15

I've been trying to set up my
IMAP for three days.

IMAP stands for Internet Message Access Protocol.
IMAP is an email system that allows you to manage
emails stored on a remote computer.

Backbone   Feb 16

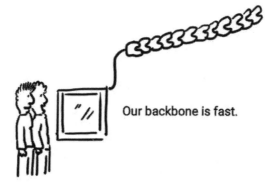

Our backbone is fast.

A backbone is a high speed wire that runs through a company.

Mashup   Feb 17

A good masher always makes a better mashup.

A Mashup is a webpage made up of embedded pages from other websites.

Client   Feb 18

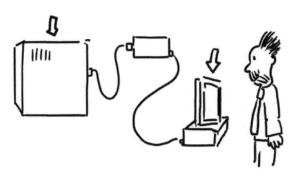

A client is usually a PC on the network. It is any computer a person uses.

Denial Of Service   Feb 19

Talk to the hand.

Denial of Service refers to overloading a website with traffic for the purpose of blocking people from using it.

FTP   Feb 20

FTP transfers files
between computers.

FTP stands for File Transfer Protocol.

ASCII   Feb 21

You look familiar.

ASCII stands for American Standard Code for
Information Interchange. ASCII goes back to when
computers didn't have graphics. Pronounced (ask key).

ODBC   Feb 22

ODBC sends
data between
computers.

ODBC stands for Open Database Connectivity. ODBC
can connect many types of databases.

Whois   Feb 23

It says my website is
owned by Tabby The Cat.

Doing a search for the word "WHOIS" brings you to many
Whois websites.

Hypermedia   Feb 24

I guess that's why it's called hypermedia.

Hypermedia is like a hyperlink. You can jump around to different videos.

Wearables   Feb 25

Yes. It's an early model wearable. But it still works.

A good example of wearables are the Apple watch and the Fitbit.

Photoshopped   Feb 26

I photoshopped my head on another body. Is it obvious?

Photoshop is a popular graphics editing program made by Adobe.

P2P   Feb 27

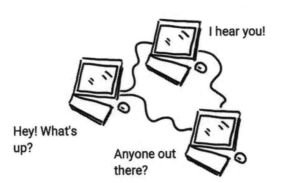

I hear you!

Hey! What's up?

Anyone out there?

P2P stands for peer-to-peer. A P2P network is when computers connect to each other and manage their own network.

CPM   Feb 28

Your click just cost
someone money.

CPM stands for Click Per Mille. Mille means thousands.
CPM is used in Internet advertising. It is how much you
pay for an ad.

TCP   Mar 1

This letter was
guaranteed to
be delivered.
Just like TCP...

TCP stands for Transmission Control Protocol. TCP
connects computers across the internet

Title Bar   Mar 2

Hold down the mouse button on the titlebar to drag it.

Double click the title bar to make it dragable.

Reboot   Mar 3

Okay. Reboot. That will give us time to make a fresh pot of coffee.

Reboot comes from the word bootstrap as in pull yourself up by the bootstraps.

Crash   Mar 4

Your computer crashed!

Make sure you have plenty of harddrive space.
Computers can crash when they run low on memory.

Analog   Mar 5

My watch is
analog.

My watch
is digital.

Analog is an estimate while digital is precise.

VOIP

Mar 6

Hello!

VOIP stands for Voice Over Internet Protocol. VOIP is when you make a phone call through your computer.

Defrag

Mar 7

I need to defrag my desk.

Defrag stands for defragment. It cleans up your drive of deleted files.

Hibernate   Mar 8

My computer is hibernating.

Your computer hibernates when it takes a rest but does not shut off.

404   Mar 9

My sock is 404.

When something is 404... it is missing.

Adware   Mar 10

This adware goes too far.

Adware is software that is free because it has advertisements in it.

DBMS   Mar 11

My DBMS replaced my filing cabinet.

DBMS stands for database management system. MySql is an example of a DBMS.

CAD   Mar 12

See what a thirty
thousand dollar CAD
system gets you?

CAD stands for Computer Aided Design.

DAAS   Mar 13

This card has your
desktop on it.

DAAS stands for Desktop As A Service. DAAS is a virtual
operating system and each computer has no disk drive.

Nixie   Mar 14

A new way to use
nixies was found.

A nixie is a drone that hovers and takes selfies of you.

Radio Button   Mar 15

I clicked the radio button
but I don't hear anything.

A radio button is an on/off button in a computer program.

Botnet   Mar 16

We're under attack by a botnet.

A botnet is a group of computer programs that has infected a lot of computers and launches virus attacks.

Command   Mar 17

WOOF!

>BARK

Good! Let's try another command.

Commands are run by using the command prompt.

Java   Mar 18

I drink java when I program Java.

Java is used to create interactive programs over the internet.

Closed Architecture   Mar 19

You can't change anything when you have a closed architecture.

A closed architecture is when a manufacturer controls what programs can be built on or run on a computer.

Cookie   Mar 20

My computer really likes cookies.

Cookies are small files that hold information about websites you visited.

DPI   Mar 21

I need a monitor with more DPI.

DPI stands for Dots Per Inch. The more dots per inch a monitor has... the better the picture is.

Concatenate   Mar 22

I found Qwerty on the keyboard!

Keyboards are called Qwerty because the upper left keys spell the word Qwerty.

Qwerty   Mar 23

I concatenate peanut butter and jelly.

Concatenate means to mix or combine.

VLE   Mar 24

Keep your hands up!

VLE stands for Virtual Learning Environment. A VLE is when you learn with a simulation that feels real.

App   Mar 25

My app says when I can drink coffee.

An app is a program that usually runs on a small device like a phone or a tablet.

Ning

Mar 26

They're my fans. I met them on Ning.

Ning allows you to make custom social networks.

Email Blast

Mar 27

Oof!

An email blast is when you send out a lot of emails at one time.

Zip

Mar 28

I zipped up your luggage.

A zip program compresses files and makes them smaller.

Selfie

Mar 29

Why is it called a sell fee if you give them away for free?

A selfie is a picture you take of yourself with your phone camera.

Ethernet   Mar 30

We have an ethernet.

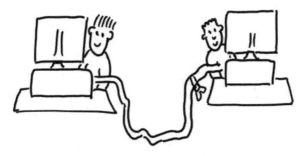

An ethernet is when you connect computers to a network.

IoT   Mar 31

I don't know how an
Internet aware
toothbrush works...
but...

IoT stands for The Internet of Things. IoT is connecting
machines to a network by using embedded computers.

In Windows... the minimize Box looks like a minus sign.

Spam is named after the luncheon meat.

Maximize   Apr 3

All I know is... I clicked
the maximize button...

In Windows... the maximize button looks like a plus sign.

Augmented Reality   Apr 4

Please tell me this
is augmented
reality...

Augmented reality is when something from the computer
appears to be part of the real world.

+1   Apr 5

+1 for the hat!
Love it!

+1 refers to liking something by pressing the like button.

Trojan Horse   Apr 6

Don't click!
It may be a
Trojan horse!

A Trojan horse is a program that acts innocent but it is up
to no good.

Latency

Apr 7

His files are late
because of the latency.

Latency is any delay on a computer. You press a button
and wait... that is latency.

Bitcoin

Apr 8

It's a bitcone.
The ice cream
is virtual.

Bitcoin is a virtual currency. It is similar to a debit card.

Brick   Apr 9

I think you're talking into a brick...

A phone is a brick when it doesn't work... especially when it won't turn on.

Boolean   Apr 10

The B button is on and the A button is off. That is boolean logic.

Boolean is when something can only be true or false.

Phishing

Apr 11

I think this may be a phishing scam.

A phishing scam is when a website appears legitimate but it is for stealing from you.

Cobol

Apr 12

Just think... the first Cobol program ever written!

Cobol is an old language used on mainframes. New programs are not developed in it.

POP Mail   Apr 13

My pop mail
is working!

POP stands for Post Office Protocol. POP Mail is an older
mail system... IMAP is newer.

SEO   Apr 14

The SEO works!
The stats prove it.

SEO stands for Search Engine Optimization. SEO is when
the traffic to a website is maximized by making the site
attractive to search engines.

Troll   Apr 15

The troll liked to leave nasty comments.

A troll is someone who is very mean to people on the Internet. Especially by leaving nasty comments in a post.

Gopro   Apr 16

I love GoPro videos!

GoPro is a wearable camera showing your point of view.

Spoof

Apr 17

I think this bird site might be a spoof.

A spoof is like a phishing scam but sometimes it is not criminal but rather mischievous.

Vaporware

Apr 18

It looks like they sold you vaporware.

Vaporware is software that was never built as promised.

Telnet   Apr 19

No! I said
telnet! Not
skynet!

Telnet allows one computer to log onto another
computer.

Chip   Apr 20

These chips are
not very tasty.

A chip is a part inside the computer. It does calculations
and carries out instructions.

Bootleg   Apr 21

Psst... want to buy an accounting system?

Bootleg means to illegally copy and share software.

Favicon   Apr 22

These are my favorite favicons... ice cream and money dot com.

A favicon is an icon pointing to a website or a URL.

CPL   Apr 23

My cost per lead is one carrot.

CPL stands for Cost Per Lead. CPL refers to a cost paid for advertising on the internet.

Avatar   Apr 24

You really do look like your avatar!

An avatar is a picture representing you on the Internet.

WAN   Apr 25

This the map of our WAN.

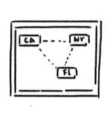

WAN stands for Wide Area Network.
A WAN is a network that runs across the world.

Edutainment   Apr 26

That is edutaining!

Edutainment is when educational content is mixed with
entertainment.

ICloud   Apr 27

The iCloud is cloud
computing for the Apple user.

Think of it as renting your own server on the Internet.

FAQ   Apr 28

Our FAQ would
soon be answered.

FAQ stands for Frequently asked Questions. An FAQ is
designed to automate the process of answering common
questions.

Telecommute — Apr 29

The lucky few can telecommute.

Telecommuting is when you work from home and share files via the Internet.

Batch Process — Apr 30

There are more batches in the hall.

A batch Process is when you process a bunch of data at the same time.

USB   May 1

We use USB on my planet too. It's universal.

USB stands for Universal Serial Bus. A USB wire transfers data to your phone or computer. It also charges it.

RAM   May 2

Now I know why they call it ram.

RAM is temporary memory used by your computer. It goes away when the computer is shut off.

ROM

May 3

I have to get a computer that doesn't only have ROM!

ROM stands for Read Only Memory. ROM is unchangeable memory. It's always there on startup.

Byte

May 4

I take a byte of data one character at a time.

A byte is made up of eight on/off switches called bits. Bytes tell the computer what to do.

Bit

May 5

I will only eat a bit of each byte.

A bit is an on-off switch inside the computer. It tells a byte what to be.

HTTP

May 6

HTTP connects computers and transfers data between them.

HTTP stands for HyperText Transfer Protocol.

Bitmap   May 7

Can you send me
a better bitmap?

A bitmap is an uncompressed image of high quality.

GPS   May 8

The GPS says we are
near the beach.

GPS stands for Global Positioning System.

Homepage

May 9

This is my homepage.

A homepage is your personal website.

Gigo

May 10

Now I know what GIGO means.

GIGO stands for Garbage In Garbage Out. If you put bad data into a program... you will get bad information from it.

Gigabytes   May 11

I have a billion gigabytes of memory. You?

I have one.

Think of a gigabyte as a big unit of memory inside the computer.

Vector Graphic   May 12

Vector graphics allows me to resize my bunnies with no loss of quality.

A vector graphic draws a picture by connecting dots. The image keeps the same quality when it's resized.

Opacity   May 13

Your menu needs less opacity.

Opacity is the ability to see through an object.

HTTPS   May 14

When you see the lock in
the browser... your
connection is secure.

HTTPS stands for Hyper Text Transfer Protocol Secure.
Never put your credit card in unless it says HTTPS.

Cross Platform   May 15

My Smiley is cross platform.

A program is cross platform if it can run on different types of computers.

End User   May 16

You're the end user... your opinion is very important.

The end user is the person who will use the program daily.

I/O   May 17

One plus one goes in
and a two comes out.

I/O stands for Input Output. Input is any data that goes
into the computer. Output is the result of what the
computer has done to the data.

Stream   May 18

Just imagine... data
moving down a stream.

When a computer moves data... it is called a stream.

FIFO   May 19

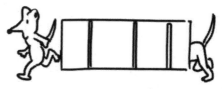

That mouse went in first
and it came out first.

FIFO stands for First In First Out. FIFO means data moves
forward like water through a hose.

Dual Boot   May 20

Will I use Linux or Windows?

Computers can start different operating systems if they
are installed.

Bluetooth   May 21

The bluetooth inventor.

Bluetooth is for exchanging data between computers over short distances.

LIFO   May 22

But... I just got here!

LIFO stands for Last In First Out. Put a card on a deck of cards. Take the card off. That is Last In First Out.

FPS

May 23

My monitor has a low FPS rate. I can only watch paint dry.

FPS stands for Frames Per Second. The higher FPS your monitor has... the easier it is on your eyes.

Emoji

May 24

I don't know why but I like that one.

Emojis are used in chat and forums to convey emotion.

GHz   May 25

I don't know but the logo
doesn't scream gigahertz.

GHz stands for Gigahertz. GHz is how fast the computer
can process data. The faster the better.

Extranet   May 26

This is our extranet.
Use it anytime.

An extranet is an internal network that can be accessed
from outside the company.

Screensaver   May 27

I'm glad you like my
Screensaver...

A Screensaver was used to protect the monitor from
being turned on for too long in the past. All it does now is
lock people out of the computer.

ISP   May 28

The ISP connects
you to the Web. It
also connects you
to businesses.

ISP stands for Internet service provider. An ISP is a
company that provides a connection to and from the
Internet.

Hashtag   May 29

People can find my cat
tweet because of the #.

A hashtag tells Twitter what search category to put your
tweet in so people can find it.

Spreadsheet   May 30

This is my pet
spreadsheet.

Microsoft Excel is an example of a spreadsheet. A
spread is like a fancy calculator.

Hub

May 31

I think we need a bigger hub.

A hub connects computers and devices to a network.

Sim Card

Jun 1

My SIM card will turn your phone into my phone.

A Sim card has information about your phone account such as your phone number.

MAC   Jun 2

The MAC address is the address of your computer on the Internet.

MAC stands for Media Access Control. The MAC address is a unique name for your computer.

Macro   Jun 3

When I click the macro... it will add the numbers and get the total.

A macro is a prerecorded program that runs commands when you click it.

URL   Jun 4

What's your favorite URL?

Cats dot com.

Dogs dot com.

URL stands for Uniform Resource Locator. A URL is an address to a resource on the Internet. An example of a resource is www.NewWordADay.com.

SMTP   Jun 5

I setup SMTP to send emails.

SEND

SMTP stands for Simple Mail Transfer Protocol. SMTP is a system that allows you to send and receive email.

SQL   Jun 6

You say
Sequel...

I say
S.Q.L. ...

Let's call the whole thing off!

SQL stands for Structured Query Language. It is used to get data from SQL databases.

Firewire   Jun 7

My computer is faster
with firewire.

Firewire is a high speed cable that connects computers and devices.

Unlocked cell phone

Jun 8

My cell phone is unlocked. I can do whatever I want with it.

An unlocked phone is not tied to a phone carrier such as Verizon or Sprint.

Acrobat

Jun 9

Here's your Adobe Acrobat file!

Adobe Acrobat is used to edit PDF documents.

Open Source — Jun 10

We have a bug in the math module. Can you fix it?

Yes. It's open source. We can change it.

An open source program is one where you get the computer code so you can make changes to the program.

Ping — Jun 11

I can ping the server. The problem is not the network.

Ping tells if you can connect to another computer and how long it takes the other computer to reply.

Certificate   Jun 12

That's the certificate
for my website.

A certificate is like a license for a website. It proves who
owns the site and that it is not a spoof.

Motherboard   Jun 13

Thanks Mom!
That's the most
important board!

The motherboard is the where the brains of the system
sits.

Control Panel

Jun 14

This is the control panel.
It controls my computer.

On a Windows system... the control panel sets the settings for your computer.

Intranet

Jun 15

I have an intranet in my garage.

An intranet is an internal network inside a business or a building.

Crop

Jun 16

I have to learn how to crop better.

You crop a picture by selecting it with a cutting tool on a computer or a phone.

Kindle

Jun 17

Maybe it's time to get a Kindle.

A Kindle is a tablet that is good for reading books.

File Extension

Jun 18

I put an extension on my house.

An extension tells you the type a file is... such as a txt extension which is a text file.

Etsy

Jun 19

It's a hair ball. I glued it on a stick. I just sold it on Etsy.

Etsy is a website where people can sell their original artwork or other original work.

Impressions   Jun 20

This makes an impression on me!

An impression is when a person on the Internet sees something on a website.

Ergonomic   Jun 21

It's silly looking but it's ergonomic.

Ergonomic means to make something have less stress on the body.

API   Jun 22

It's the latest API.
No hands needed.

API stands for Application Program Interface. An API gives a programmer a way to send custom commands to a program.

Linux   Jun 23

You say
Line-ex...

I say Lin-ex...

Let's call the whole thing off!

Linux is a free operating system that runs a computer.

TMI   Jun 24

Oh my! That's TMI!

TMI stands for Too Much Informaion. TMI means you've heard or seen something you'd rather not have seen.

Logfile   Jun 25

I always keep a logfile.

A logfile records activity on the computer. It is like a history of what a program has done.

IP   Jun 26

You don't need an IP address on your business card.

IP stands for Internet Protocol. An IP address is the public address of a computer or a device.

I.T.   Jun 27

I'm from I.T.. We heard you have an illegal cat screensaver.

I.T. stands for Information Technology. The I.T. Department is usually the computer department of a company.

Blogosphere

Jun 28

I'm going to the blogosphere.

The blogosphere is what the world of blogs is called on the Internet.

PDF5

Jun 29

Your PDF prints better than my regular document.

PDF stands for Portable Document Format. A PDF looks like a printed document on the screen.

Num Lock   Jun 30

Turn the num lock
on. You can enter
numbers faster
than pecking on
the keyboard.

Num Lock stands for Number Lock. The extended keys
are used for data entering numbers.

Null   Jul 1

Not null!

Null!

A null equals nothing. When you see a null it means
nothing has ever been there.

Hard Token   Jul 2

By the time I type the number... it changes. Now I know why it's called a hard token... it's too hard.

A hard token gives you a temporary password that matches a password you are being asked for.

White Balance   Jul 3

I think you need to adjust the white balance on your camera.

White Balance is when you adjust the brightness of white on an image to make it look better.

Pixel   Jul 4

It's my artistic invention...
the one pixel painting.

One dot on the screen is a pixel.

PPL   Jul 5

These are my PPL. They
are my friends.

PPL stands for "people" and it's used in chat and in
email.

Cell

Jul 6

Psst! Hey! Grab that key and let me out! Will ya!?

A cell is one rectangle in a spreadsheet. It usually contains numbers.

Status Bar

Jul 7

The status bar gives you information about the program.

Remote Desktop — Jul 8

I just remoted in. You might want to close what you're working on.

Remote Desktop allows someone to see your computer screen and control your keyboard and mouse.

Emoticon — Jul 9

I'm working as an emoticon... but I'm really an actor.

An emoticon is used to show people what mood you are in.

Hyperlink   Jul 10

I'm so hyper! I think I'll click a link!

Hyper comes from the Greek word huper which means beyond or over as in overflow.

SDK   Jul 11

I used the SDK to make the link to the other program.

SDK stands for Software Development Kit. An SDK allows you to build custom programs for computer software.

Keyword

Jul 12

I don't think "monkey" is a good keyword for a cat website.

Keywords are embedded in a website to tell the search engines how to find your site.

Mi-Fi

Jul 13

I'm sorry you brought your Mi-FI.

Mi-Fi stands for Mobile Wi-Fi. MI-FI is like carrying a building or house Internet connection with you.

Minisite   Jul 14

My minisite is about Pirate Cats.
I admit I don't get many visitors.

A minisite is a small website usually dedicated to
unpopular topics.

Zine   Jul 15

My zine is all about spoons.

A zine is a small online magazine usually dedicated to
one topic.

Footprint

Jul 16

Your monitor has
a tiny footprint.

A footprint is the space something takes up on your
desk.

Third Party

Jul 17

He's our third-party
developer. Don't let his
looks fool you.

A third-party developer is an outside company who
builds software you add to a program you are making.

GUI

Jul 18

This screen is all gooey!

Hmm... interesting name. That's what I'll name my new Invention.

GUI stands for Graphical User Interface. A GUI is the screen and its forms.

Truncate

Jul 19

Who truncated my candy bar?

Truncate means to reduce something in size.

BTW   Jul 20

BTW...
love the
hat.

BTW... love
the shirt.

BTW stands for "By The Way". BTW is used in chat and
email to change the subject.

WYSIWYG   Jul 21

This 3D maker says it's WYSIWYG.
I don't get it...

WYSIWYG stands for "What You See Is What You Get".
WYSIWYG pronounced Wiz-ee-wig - means what you
see on the screen is what the output will be.

Ajax

Jul 22

They said to use Ajax... but now it's not working.

Ajax is for programmers to update only parts of a website without refreshing the whole webpage.

XML

Jul 23

I need a database but I also want a text file.

Sounds like XML!

An XML file is a text file that has field names in it so it can also be read by a database.

Blu-Ray   Jul 24

As you can see... the Blu-Ray
on the right has a clearer
picture than the regular DVD.

A Blu-Ray is like a DVD but with higher quality.

3D Printer   Jul 25

I don't know what it is...
but 3D printing is amazing.

A 3D printer allows you to draw realistic things and
build them in melted plastic.

Debug   Jul 26

This is how I debug a program.

You debug a program by fixing the errors and problems.

Digitize   Jul 27

I'm digitizing the photo now.

A photo is digitized by converting it to computer pixels.

Bot

Jul 28

A bot has taken over my computer!

A bot is a program that goes from computer to computer and does bad things. It often reports back to its owner much like a robot.

Basic

Jul 29

You must be our Basic programmer.

BASIC stands for Beginner's All-Purpose Symbolic Instruction Code.

Binary

Jul 30

A light switch is binary. It is either on or off.

Something that is binary... can only be on or off. True or false is also binary. Yes and no is binary too.

Cyberspace

Jul 31

I live in cyberspace.

Cyberspace is the total of the Internet. It is the imaginary world of games and websites.

Drag and Drop — Aug 1

I did say drag and drop...

In Windows... you drag and drop by holding the left mouse button down allowing you to grab things such as a window. The item is dropped when you release the mouse button.

Cybersquatter — Aug 2

I need to use my computer. Can you televisionsquat for a while?

A cybersquatter buys a website with no intention of using it... in the hopes of selling it later.

Google Drive   Aug 3

Don't email files between computers. Drop them in your Google drive and pick them up on the other computer.

A Google drive is a virtual drive in the cloud. You can drop files in it like a local drive.

Client Server   Aug 4

The server serves data to the client.

Your computer is a client on the network and bigger computers that control the network and the data are the servers.

A/B Testing   Aug 5

I think people are going to choose the carrot over the stick.

A/B Testing presents two webpages to users to see which one they will like best.

Linkedin   Aug 6

Tabby has many Linkedin connections.

Linkedin is a site dedicated to meeting other people to help your business networking or job search.

Post   Aug 7

Well... I did say post a reply.

You post to the Internet when you upload content to a website... especially a comment or opinion.

Sandbox   Aug 8

Not that kind of a sandbox...

A sandbox is a protected part of your computer where programs can run without getting access to your personal drive.

Redirect   Aug 9

I went to a cat site and ended up here.

A redirect occurs when a website sends you to another website without your knowledge.

Clickbait   Aug 10

Don't click it! It's clickbait!

Clickbait is a link that promises something interesting but delivers something self-serving.

Alt Text   Aug 11

The second cat picture is missing. I can click the link anyway.

Alt Text is the text that appears on a Web page when a picture is missing. You can still click it and follow the link.

AFK   Aug 12

I forgot to say AFK!

BOARD⇒

AFK means Away From Keyboard. It is used in chat and email.

Viral   Aug 13

Look! Your picture went viral!

Viral means something is spreading across the
Internet from person to person... like a virus.

Wordpress   Aug 14

I use
WordPress
for my
website.

I use
WordPress
to blog.

WordPress is a popular free site for making blogs and
websites.

Encryption   Aug 15

This is the Encryption Department.

Encryption stops other people from reading your files.

WordArt   Aug 16

I think your WordArt is better my art.

WordArt is the clipart found in Microsoft Word.

Instagram   Aug 17

Hey! That looks familiar!

Instagram allows you to take a photo and instantly share it. It also has funny filters that edit photos in real-time.

Permalink   Aug 18

I said permanent link... not permanent ink.

Permalink stands for Permanent Link. A permanent link is the originating page of a photo or an article. People can count on using it because it will never be changed.

Click And Mortar   Aug 19

I buy it online and I pick it up here.

Click and Mortar is when you buy something online and pick it up at a local store.

Javascript   Aug 20

Javascript is like Java but light. So... I only drink decaf.

Javascript is a scripting language. It extends the power of a website and allows the website to become a program.

Frame

Aug 21

That's the first time I've seen a frame in a frame.

Frames are like mini-pages on a website.

Boss Key

Aug 22

The boss key is the biggest and most important key.

A boss key is a key on the keyboard that hides your screen... you click it when the boss is coming.

WWW

Aug 23

People get trapped in the WWW.

WWW stands for World Wide Web. It is also called the Internet.

Meme

Aug 24

Don't move! This will be a great meme!

A meme is a funny image or video that has gone viral.

IRL   Aug 25

I'm glad this isn't IRL.

IRL means In Real Life.

Launch   Aug 26

That's what I call a
successful launch!

A launch refers to a new software launch. It is like a
grand opening.

Dox

Aug 27

I got doxed! That's my underwear on the Internet for all the world to see!

You dox someone by telling their secrets on the Internet.

Data Warehouse

Aug 28

What is a data warehouse?

A data warehouse is made of many databases.

A data warehouse tends not to move data around but rather compiles data from different sources.

Bloatware   Aug 29

This program is bloatware!

Bloarware is software with too many features. It takes a long time to run and may get memory problems.

Nagware   Aug 30

BUY!
SAVE

This program keeps nagging me to buy something.

Nagware is free software that constantly asks you to purchase something.

Modular

Aug 31

Can you make these changes?

Yes. The program is modular. We can change any module.

A modular program is made up of mini-programs. Mini-programs can be changed without affecting the entire program.

WMV

Sep 1

This is my favorite WMV!

WMV stands for Windows Media Video. A WMV is a movie file that originated on the Windows operating system.

Smiley   Sep 2

The smiley was the start of emojis.

The smiley is used usually at the end of an email or chat to show happiness.

Microblogging   Sep 3

You must be the head of microblogging.

A microblog is a short and small blog. It is often updated during the day.

Moodle   Sep 4

I think we're going to like this site!

Moodle stands for Modular Object-Oriented Dynamic Learning Environment. Moodle is a free website for teachers to make courses.

Crowd Funding   Sep 5

I'm using Crowd Funding for my new business.

Crowd Funding is when you raise money for a business idea or project from people on the Internet. You give them stuff in exchange for their money... such as a signed product.

Legacy

Sep 6

I think it's time to replace that legacy monitor.

Legacy is any technology that is old and generally not bought anymore.

String

Sep 7

No... I meant send me a data string.

A string refers to a string of data. A data string is any combination of letters and numbers.

Showstopper — Sep 8

This may be a showstopper...

A showstopper is a bug or a problem that stops a program from going live.

Disruptive — Sep 9

The IPhone was disruptive technology for the flip phone.

Disruptive technology replaces an old technology. The car was disruptive technology for the buggy whip.

Propagate

Sep 10

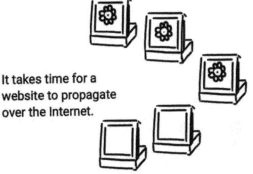

It takes time for a website to propagate over the Internet.

A website or a program propagates across the Internet as server after server picks it up and makes copies of it.

Shareware

Sep 11

I know it's shareware but we don't have to share the keyboard.

A shareware program is given away for free with the intent of making money from it in the future.

B2B   Sep 12

Okay. I will send the file
and wait for your system
to process it. B2B is
great!

B2B means Business To Business.

Site Map   Sep 13

I find this Site Map confusing.

A site map gives you directions to the features on a
website.

Applet

Sep 14

My little phone can only run applets.

Applets are small apps or programs usually for a phone or tablet. They are often limited in function.

Softcopy

Sep 15

No! A softcopy is electronic... it's not a piece of paper.

A softcopy is an electronic version of a document.

Hard Copy   Sep 16

I want a paper hardcopy.. not chiseled rock.

A hardcopy is a printed paper version of a document.

Bandwith   Sep 17

I need more bandwidth. All I can play is Snail Attack.

Bandwidth is the speed of a network. The more bandwidth the network has... the faster data will go.

IMHO — Sep 18

IMHO... the plaid pants have to go.

IMHO stands for "In My Humble Opinion".

E-Learning — Sep 19

Hey! You graduated your e-learning class!

E-learning is when you learn a topic over the Internet. You can earn degrees and certifications.

Mime

Sep 20

That's not the mime
I had in mind.

MIME stands for Multi-Purpose Internet Mail
Extensions.

Specs

Sep 21

Here are the specs you asked for.

Spec is short for specifications. A specification is a
design or a set of instructions on how a program should
be built.

Netiquette

Sep 22

Your netiquette is terrible.

Netiquette is how you behave on the Internet.

Node

Sep 23

NODE 1

NODE 5

A computer is a node on a network.

Every device or computer is a node on a network.

Ebook

Sep 24

I see you got the best selling ebook about sheep.

Ebooks are electronic and virtual books. The Kindle is a popular Ebook reader.

CMB

Sep 25

Please CMB. I'll have to talk to you later.

CMB stands for "Call Me Back".

Freeware — Sep 26

It may be free but it doesn't do much.

Freeware is free software given away because it acts as a loss leader for another product.

HDTV — Sep 27

The clarity of this HDTV is amazing.

HDTV stands for High Definition Television.

Pinterest

Sep 28

Maybe it's time you used Pinterest.

Pinterest is a website for sharing photos.

NAGI

Sep 29

It's NAGI to give your credit card to someone you don't know on the internet..

NAGI stands for "Not A Good Idea".

Skyscraper   Sep 30

The skyscraper ads
are a little much.

A skyscraper ad is a long tall ad often taking up a lot
of space.

IOS   Oct 1

It's called IOS
because it runs on
an iPhone. Glad
it's not called
pPhone.

The OS stands for "Operating System". No one knows
what the i stands for... Only Steve Jobs knew...

Asynchronous   Oct 2

Asynchronous talking makes you a good listener and a good talker.

Asynchronous means to wait for something else to finish before doing something.

Mainframe   Oct 3

This is our mainframe. We don't know who built it or when we got it.

A mainframe is a very big powerful computer.

Scroll Wheel
Oct 4

This is the greatest scroll wheel ever!

A scroll wheel is often included on a mouse. You use your finger to make it scroll the screen up or down.

Burn
Oct 5

I burned a new CD for you.

You burn a CD when you copy files to it.

Illegal Operation   Oct 6

That's an illegal operation!

An illegal operation is when you try to do something the computer can't understand. Dividing by zero is an illegal operation because it is impossible.

PUP   Oct 7

FLAPPY IS INSTALLED!

What the heck is Flappy!?

PUP stands for Potentially Unwanted Program. PUP is a program that installed itself without your permission.

PLZ   Oct 8

Always use the magic word!

PLZ is short for Please. It is used in chat and email.

L8R   Oct 9

L8R is short for Later in chat and email.

Internet

Oct 10

Remember... the internet is made up of connected networks.

Inter stands for Interconnected... Net stands for Networks. InterNet = Interconnected Networks.

Bump

Oct 11

There! My good comment will bump your comment to the top.

Websites move a post to the top of the webpage when someone leaves a comment. Writing the word Bump moves the post to the top.

Plug-in   Oct 12

The Amazon Assistant plug-in always finds good prices!

A plug-in is a program that runs in your browser. It can do things for you while you surf the net.

Read Only   Oct 13

You lie! You could not have saved the file! It was read only!

A read only file cannot be changed. Often a password is required to make it writable.

Canoe

Oct 14

A tweet can start a Twitter Canoe.

A Twitter Canoe is when a bunch of people are involved in a Twitter conversation. Often... the extra people are unwanted.

Peripheral

Oct 15

A coffee maker is my favorite peripheral.

A peripheral is a device attached to your computer or your network.

Snapchat   Oct 16

You'll find no evidence...
I use Snapchat.

Snapchat can send messages that will automatically be deleted after being read by the recipient.

C   Oct 17

I knew it was written in C... but I didn't expect it to run on my blender.

C is a cross platform language that can make a program that runs on any computer.

Blog   Oct 18

I'm blogging right now... about people who annoy me while I'm blogging.

A blog is like a public interactive diary. You can post your thoughts that people can reply.

Tweet   Oct 19

All you do is sit around and tweet all day.

A tweet is a post on Twitter. A post on Twitter is a micro-blog.

Facebook   Oct 20

I think Facebook is
better than Footbook.

Facebook allows you to connect with friends and
family and exchange all sorts of things.

PHP   Oct 21

I don't like
PHP...

Facebook was
built in it.

I meant to
say I like
PHP...

PHP is a computer language used to create
webpages.

Spyware — Oct 22

Spyware is software that records your screen and keystrokes. It is used to secretly watch your computer activity.

Copy and Paste — Oct 23

I love to copy and paste chew toys.

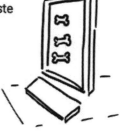

Copy and paste allows you to duplicate images and text on the screen.

Chat Room   Oct 24

Hey all!
What's up!?

A chat room is a webpage where you can talk to other people.

Upload   Oct 25

Stand back! The upload has started!

An upload is when you send a local file to a website by using an upload menu.

Vlogger   Oct 26

You want to make a vlog about me?

Just did.

A vlog is a video blog.

Camelcase   Oct 27

Yes. I always use camelcase. How did you know?

Camel case is a way to make concatenated words stand out. The first letter in each word is capitalized. The word oatmeal becomes OatMeal when camel case is used.

Moderator

Oct 28

Okay you two! I'll decide who is right!

A moderator decides if people are being nice to each other when posting something in the comment section of a website.

Wiki

Oct 29

Aloha Wiki! Teach me!

Wiki comes from the Hawaiian language and it means quick.

Podcast   Oct 30

His pod is where he does his podcast.

A podcast is like a radio show except it runs over the Internet instead of the airwaves.

Worksheet   Oct 31

You only need a keyboard for a worksheet.

A worksheet is a page inside a spreadsheet.

Upgrade   Nov 1

I upgraded my
monitor to 3D.

Software can be upgraded by installing a new version
of it from the Internet. An upgrade usually fixes bugs
and makes improvements.

Formula   Nov 2

FRUIT =
APPLES +
ORANGES

This formula is perfect!

A formula can be typed into a spreadsheet, a
calculator or a program.

AWS   Nov 3

I use AWS for my pet website.

I use AWS for my entire pet business.

AWS stands for Amazon Web Services. It is a huge suite of cloud based business tools.

Autostart   Nov 4

Why does a pic of a fish autostart on my computer?

You can set a program to autostart every time the computer starts.

Bookmark — Nov 5

You can bookmark something on the Internet or inside a program. You can return to your previous location by clicking the bookmark.

Catfish — Nov 6

A catfish is a person who uses a fake identity online.

Webcam   Nov 7

It was a bad time to learn
the new Webcam was on.

A Webcam is a camera that lets you send a video of
yourself over the Internet in real-time.

Format   Nov 8

The format command deletes everything from your
hard drive... permanently.

Forum

Nov 9

You dressed to chat in the forum?

A forum is a chat room on a website.

Hardware

Nov 10

This is our hardware section.

The computer itself is called "hardware". The program that runs the computer is called "software".

Autosum
Nov 11

Something is wrong with the autosum.

Autosum is when a spreadsheet adds all the numbers in a column and gives you a total.

Tag
Nov 12

I'm going to tag you in this photo.

A tag is used on Facebook to identify people in uploaded photos.

Real-Time   Nov 13

She knew where he was in real-time.

Real-time means instant or up to the minute and with no delay.

Glassdoor   Nov 14

Use Glassdoor to learn what's behind it.

BIGCO

Glass door is a website that rates and reviews companies from the point of view of the employees.

Organic Search   Nov 15

That's an organic search!

An organic search is a search where none of the search results are ads or paid for. They are real results.

Firmware   Nov 16

Firmware is firm. It rarely changes.

Firmware is software that is embedded in the hardware. .

CNBU   Nov 17

CNBU stands for Can Not Be Unseen.

ROFL   Nov 18

ROFL stands for "Roll On the Floor Laughing".

PrtScrn   Nov 19

Why is it called Print Screen if it just copies the screen to the clipboard?

PrntScrn is short for Print Screen. In Windows... the prntscrn button copies the screen into the clipboard and it can be copy and pasted into a program.

Registry   Nov 20

You touched the registry again... didn't you...

The registry in Windows is the main configuration file for the computer. You should never touch this file because it can damage the system.

Tab   Nov 21

Maybe this program should
be more than two tabs...

Tabs allow programs to have multiple screens on
one screen.

Look and Feel   Nov 22

It does have a dog look and feel.

Look and Feel refers to the style of a website and
what the user experience is.

Eye Tracking   Nov 23

The eye tracking proves people like ice cream better than broccoli.

Eye tracking is when the computer watches your eyes to see where you are looking on the screen.

Snail Mail   Nov 24

Your check is in the snail mail... I mean the mail.

Snail Mail refers to putting a letter in an envelope and mailing it through the Post Office.

Descending Order   Nov 25

You're right. Descending order shows me the bigger number.

Sorting by Descending Order is when you tell a spreadsheet to list the numbers in a column by the larger numbers first.

User Friendly   Nov 26

My! This is a user friendly program!

A program is user friendly when it is easy to understand and it is easy to use.

Wallpaper   Nov 27

Frankly... your choice of
wallpaper creeps me out.

Wallpaper is the image that sits on the background
of your computer.

Word Wrap   Nov 28

I did tell you to
use word wrap.

Word Wrap is when a program keeps all the text on
the screen by wrapping each sentence onto the next
line.

PMJI   Nov 29

PMJI... Would you like my opinion?

PMJI stands for "Pardon My Jumping In".

Skype   Nov 30

Tabby liked to Skype all day long.

Skype is a program that lets you video chat and text chat with other people.

Developer   Dec 1

I developed a DBMS for Microsoft... and... Flappy Fish.

A developer is someone who designs and builds computer programs.

IPod   Dec 2

I'll buy a new IPod when this thing fails.

An IPod lets you store and play thousands of songs.

TOS

Dec 3

The Terms Of Service are signed in blood.

TOS stands for "Terms Of Service". A TOS is the contract you have to agree to before you can use a website or a program.

Embed

Dec 4

That was fast!

It was easy. Everything is embedded from other websites.

You can embed items from other websites when they have embed code. You copy and paste it into your website.

Language

Dec 5

I gave up HTML and starting speaking French with my computer.

A computer language tells the computer what to do. You write your commands in English and a compiler turns it into machine language.

WTG

Dec 6

WTG! Woot! Woot!

WTG stands for "Way To Go". WTG is used in chat and email.

G2G   Dec 7

G2G is an acronym for "Got To Go".

ActiveX   Dec 8

ActiveX gives a website the ability to run a program. You should only allow ActiveX when you trust the website.

Blog Roll   Dec 9

A blogroll is a list of blogs that scroll down the screen.

MP3   Dec 10

MP3 stands for Motion Picture Layer 3. MP3 is a music and video file format.

NOYB   Dec 11

What's in the box? NOYB.

NOYB stands for "None Of Your Business".

Webinar   Dec 12

The Webinair
soon began.

A Webinair is a way for someone to video chat with a lot of people.

Toaster
Dec 13

I think my computer is a toaster.
Maybe it's time for a new one.

A computer is called a toaster when it is very old.
The joke being... it is so old... it is only good for
making toast.

Widget
Dec 14

I have a widget that tells me
when it's the first of the month.

A widget is like an app except it often does one task.

Wizard   Dec 15

Do you always wear a hat when you use a wizard?

A wizard is a series of menus that take you through an install or configuration process.

Feature Creep   Dec 16

Not for nothing... but you're always adding new features.

Feature Creep is the adding of new things for a program to do as it is being built. The features are unplanned and cause launch delays.

Back Slash   Dec 17

A back slash
leans to the left.

A back slash is used to denote a subfolder on a
computer. Such as... C:\CATS

Forward Slash   Dec 18

A forward slash
leans to the right.

A forward slash is used to denote a subpage on a
website. Such as NewWordADay.com/subscribe.htm

TY   Dec 19

TY!

TY stands for "Thank You".

Funnel   Dec 20

An ad funnel sends customers to a buy webpage.

A funnel steers Internet users to page after page until they land on an action page that asks them to buy something.

ASL   Dec 21

ASL stands for Age, Sex and Location. ASL is something you ask someone on the Internet when you are trying to find out more about who they are.

Compile   Dec 22

I just compiled the new version.
You can use it in a minute.

You write instructions in English for a computer. You run a program to translate the instructions into machine Language. This is called compiling.

TTYL   Dec 23

Gotta go! TTYL.

TTYL stands for "Talk To You Later".

Alpha Test   Dec 24

This is an Alpha test.
End users don't get it
yet.

An Alpha test is the fist round of testing and the
end users are not involved yet.

Beta Test   Dec 25

I see you're enjoying our Beta test.

A beta test is the second round of testing. It now involves the end users.

Biometrics   Dec 26

Your biometrics are a bit strange.

Biometrics is the measuring of the human body using computer systems.

User Persona   Dec 27

This is my user persona.
Kind of my alter ego.

A user persona is how you make yourself look to
the world on the Internet.

Frontend   Dec 28

Remember... the frontend is the
program. The backend is the data.

The frontend is the screen and the menus.

Kluge

Dec 29

This program is a kluge.
Only a child can use it.

A kluge is a poorly built program.

NSFW

Dec 30

Oh my! He said it was NSFW!

NSFW stands for "Not Safe For Work".

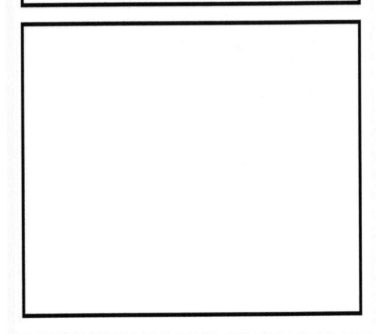

Made in the USA
San Bernardino, CA
29 December 2018